Preparing *for* Marriage

PREPARING *for* MARRIAGE

The Premarital Counsel of John Calvin

EDITED BY SCOTT T. BROWN

MERCHANT ADVENTURERS
Wake Forest, NC

OTHER BOOKS BY SCOTT BROWN

A Church in the House

Restoring Daily Worship to the Christian Household

How does a father lead his family as a shepherd of his household? In this sermon delivered in 1704, Matthew Henry explains how fathers can fulfill divine commands for fathers in their family life.

Edited by Scott Brown.

Feminine by Design

The Twelve Pillars of Biblical Womanhood

How does a young girl learn what it means to be a woman? The world needs Christ-loving, husband-helping, home-making, dominion-taking, kingdom-advancing women. The "Twelve Pillars" show the way.

Second Printing: October 2009

MERCHANT ADVENTURERS, INC.
3721 Quarry Rd Wake Forest, North Carolina 27587
www.NCFIC.org

ISBN-10: 0-9820567-2-9
ISBN-13: 978-0-9820567-2-1

Cover Design by Ryan Glick
Book Design by David Brown

Printed in the United States of America

TABLE OF CONTENTS

INTRODUCTION

This book captures some of the premarital counsel which John Calvin gave to the youth and families of Geneva. It draws from two categories of Calvin's writings, bringing up interesting and helpful counsel for young people and their families in order to help them navigate the single years and enter successfully into marriage. First, we have taken statements from his commentaries and sermons on matters relating to this formative time of a young person's life. Second, many of the statements presented here come from the Marriage Ordinance of 1546, which outlines various difficult issues that most singles need to face before they get married.

"Marriage is honorable among all, and the bed undefiled; but fornicators and adulterers God will judge."

~ Hebrews 13:4

CHAPTER ONE

A Strategic Time of Life

How young people use the years of their youth is critical for the foundation of their marriages. Poor navigational choices during the headwaters of the single years can cause a host of problems downstream. Seemingly small sins committed in the streams of youth become gigantic boulders later on that can break up the watercraft and send them hurtling rudderless over the falls. John Calvin realized this and throughout his ministry provided detailed counsel on very important matters for single people.

Premarital Books Then and Now

If you survey the content of modern books on the subject of marriage preparation, courtship, and engagement, many of the same themes of which Calvin spoke are there. Generally, modern books are grappling with two things: the culture and the teaching of Scripture. They identify the destructive practices of the surrounding culture compared to the often countercultural message of Scripture. They answer practical questions regarding romance, the dangers of the current dating system, and the false philosophies in existence today. They address matters of expectations, purity, process, and parental involvement. Calvin addressed many of these same core issues. Of course he had some slightly different cultural features to address, but the same core problems existed in Geneva as do today.

Pastoral Care for Singles in Geneva

As a shepherd of a local flock, it is evident that Calvin had observed many of the tumultuous results of mishandling the single years. He seemed to have great compassion for the single people in his church for he provided much counsel to assist them in governing the critical years preceeding marriage. He preached directly to the issues which they faced and dealt forthrightly with concerns they had regarding marriage and everything leading up to it. He did not provide them with shallow platitudes. Rather, he gave incisive direction for handling a diverse range of complex issues. Through his expositions, letters, commentaries, and the Institutes, he dissected the issues of the single life.

The Marriage Ordinance of 1546

In the Marriage Ordinance of 1546, Calvin outlined various difficult issues that most singles need to face before they get married. The ordinance covered controversial issues such as who could marry without permission, what to do in the case of a reckless promise of marriage, and how to handle cases of deception. The Marriage Ordinance was used by the city government as a legal guideline for settling disputes and establishing practices which reflected the teaching of Scripture on various matters.

Marriage Was Heartily Encouraged

Calvin's historical moment required him to speak to the issue of celibacy. The prevailing philosophy in Calvin's day devalued marriage and exalted vows of chastity resulting in a society in which twenty-five percent of the population had taken oaths of celibacy. He believed that the young people in his community needed to be rescued from this philosophy and he urged them to embrace marriage, making it clear that vows of celibacy were wicked and unscriptural. While he was privately writing letters to nuns to convince them of the evils of monastic life, he was publicly appealing to the young people in his congregation to get married. Like in our own day, he faced a culture which imperiled its youth by devaluing and unnecessarily delaying marriage.

The Process Mattered

Calvin made it clear that the process of getting married mattered. He held that there were many important issues to consider. For example, he maintained that parental consent was indispensable and that biblical principles governed the manner and form of the marriage proposal, as well as the wedding ceremony. Calvin was careful to explain the rules for marriages within families, defining the nature of what is and is not incest.

A Call for Examination of Potential Spouses

He explained what he believed to be the ins and outs of unequal yoking, the right and wrong age for marriage, the right and wrong reasons for marrying, and the role of parental authority and involvement in choosing a spouse. He argued passionately that purity needed to be protected. This type of detailed examination encouraged couples to identify various relationships which needed to be ordered correctly before marriage to insure success after marriage.

Wedding Announcements and Wedding Days

The Marriage Ordinance contains Calvin's guidelines for what to do after the engagement, for wedding announcements, and for how to conduct the marriage celebration.

Bad Behavior of Parents

Calvin also dealt with unsavory situations where there was negligence or excessive strictness of fathers who withhold marriage for wrong reasons. He also clearly opposed forced marriages, stating, "[L]et no father compel his children [to be married]."

Heartbreaking Situations

While Calvin communicated a biblical approach to marriage, he also recognized that some would encounter heartbreaking situations. For this reason, Calvin was careful to address many difficult and confusing situations such as false and rash promises of marriage. Perhaps the young bride would wake up after their wedding day only to discover something very wrong of which she knew nothing before the wedding. What was she to do if she woke to find that her new husband had disappeared for no apparent reason? What should be done when there are quarrels after a wedding? In all these situations, Calvin sought to communicate to the single people in his congregation that biblical principles governed premarital and marital life.

Was Calvin Correct in All His Pre-Marital Counsel?

We may not agree with all of Calvin's conclusions, but we do well to grapple with the issues he deals with our Bibles in hands. All of us are called to be "Bereans" who "were more noble than those in Thessalonica, in that they received the word with all readiness of mind, and searched the Scriptures daily, whether those things were so" (Acts 17:11).

This book attempts to document Calvin's counsel on many difficult and controversial matters. Use this book as a jump start for biblical research. Check the footnotes. Study the biblical texts. Instead of taking Calvin as Gospel, keep to the Gospel. And remember, Scripture is sufficient

JOHN CALVIN'S

Counsel for Critical Issues of Premarital Life

"Therefore a man shall leave his father and mother and be joined to his wife, and they shall become one flesh."

~ Genesis 2:24

CHAPTER TWO

The Importance of Marriage

Argument Against Singleness

Thus it is that God, by fearful examples, punishes the audacity of men, when, unmindful of their infirmity, they, against nature, affect that which has been denied to them, and despising the remedies which the Lord has placed in their hands, are confident in their ability to overcome the disease of incontinence by contumacious obstinacy. For what other name can we give it, when a man, admonished of his need of marriage, and of the remedy with which the Lord has thereby furnished, not only despises it, but binds himself by an oath to despise it?[1]

Not Profitable to Be Alone

It is not good that the man should be alone… - Genesis 2:18

"Non est bonum ut sit Adam solus." [This is a variation from Calvin's text, which has man instead of Adam; as the English version has. The word stands for both. As a proper name, it means Adam; as an appellation, it belongs to the human species; as an adjective, it means red; and, with a slight alteration, it signifies the ground. — Ed.] *Moses now explains the design of God in creating the woman; namely, that there should be human beings on the earth who might cultivate mutual society between themselves. Yet a doubt may arise whether this design ought to be extended to progeny, for the words simply mean that since it was not expedient for man to be alone, a wife must be created, who might be his helper. I, however, take the meaning to be this, that God begins, indeed, at the first step of human society, yet designs to include others, each*

in its proper place. The commencement, therefore, involves a general principle, that man was formed to be a social animal. "Principium ergo generale est, conditum esse hominem ut sit sociale animal." Now, the human race could not exist without the woman; and, therefore, in the conjunction of human beings, that sacred bond is especially conspicuous, by which the husband and the wife are combined in one body, and one soul; as nature itself taught Plato, and others of the sounder class of philosophers, to speak. But although God pronounced, concerning Adam, that it would not be profitable for him to be alone, yet I do not restrict the declaration to his person alone, but rather regard it as a common law of man's vocation, so that everyone ought to receive it as said to himself, that solitude is not good, excepting only him whom God exempts as by a special privilege.[2]

Is It Best to Be Married or Single?

But here another question presents itself, for these words of Paul have some appearance of inconsistency with the words of the Lord, in Genesis 2:18, where he declares, that it is not good for a man to be without a wife. What the Lord there pronounces to be evil Paul here declares to be good. I answer, that in so far as a wife is a help to her husband, so as to make his life happy, that is in accordance with God's institution; for in the beginning God appointed it so, that the man without the woman was, as it were, but half a man, and felt himself destitute of special and necessary assistance, and the wife is, as it were, the completing of the man. Sin afterwards came in to corrupt that institution of God; for in place of so great a blessing there has been substituted a grievous punishment, so that marriage is the source and occasion of many miseries. Hence, whatever evil or inconvenience there is in marriage, that arises from the corruption of the divine institution. Now, although there are in the meantime some remains still existing of the original blessing, so that a single life is often much more unhappy than the married life; yet, as married persons are involved in many inconveniences, it is with good reason that Paul teaches that it would be good for a man to abstain. In this way, there is no concealment of the troubles that are attendant upon marriage; and yet, in the meantime, there is no countenance given to those profane jests which are commonly in vogue with a view to bring it into discredit, such as the following: that a wife is a necessary evil, and that a wife is one of the greatest evils. For such sayings as these have come from Satan's workshop, and have a direct tendency to brand with disgrace God's holy institution.[3]

Christ's High View of Marriage

And the third day there was a marriage in Cana of Galilee; and the mother of Jesus was there: And both Jesus was called, and his disciples, to the marriage. - John 2:1-2

It was probably one of Christ's near relations who married a wife; for Jesus is mentioned as having accompanied his mother... It is a high honor given to marriage, that Christ not only deigned to be present at a nuptial banquet, but honored it with his first miracle.[4]

Prohibition of Marriage — an Idea for Heretics

Paul terms the prohibition of marriage a doctrine of devils (1 Tim. 4:1, 3); and the Spirit elsewhere declares that "marriage is honourable in all" (Heb. 13:4). Having afterwards interdicted their priests from marriage, [the Romanists] insist on this as a true and genuine interpretation of Scripture, though nothing can be imagined more alien to it. Should any one venture to open his lips in opposition, he will be judged a heretic, since the determination of the Church is without challenge, and it is unlawful to have any doubt as to the accuracy of her interpretation.[5]

"I have made a covenant with my eyes; Why then should I look upon a young woman?"

~ Job 31:1-4

CHAPTER THREE

Purity

Guard Against All Uncleanness

Thou shalt not commit adultery. - Exodus 20:14

> *The purport of this commandment is, that as God loves chastity and purity, we ought to guard against all uncleanness. The substance of the commandment therefore is, that we must not defile ourselves with any impurity or libidinous excess. To this corresponds the affirmative, that we must regulate every part of our conduct chastely and continently. The thing expressly forbidden is adultery, to which lust naturally tends, that its filthiness (being of a grosser and more palpable form, in as much as it casts a stain even on the body) may dispose us to abominate every form of lust.*[1]

Youth Is a Slippery Period

And Shechem spake unto his father Hamor, saying, Get me this damsel to wife. - Genesis 34:4

> *In this place it is more clearly expressed, that Shechem desired to have Dinah for his wife; for his lust was not so unbridled, that when he had defiled, he despised her... For though he had basely fallen through the precipitate ardor of lust, yet now returning to himself, he follows the guidance of nature. So much the more ought young men to take heed to themselves, lest in the slippery period of their age, the lusts of the flesh should impel them to many crimes. For, at this day, greater license everywhere prevails, so that no moderation restrains youths from shameful conduct.*[2]

"Husbands, love your wives, just as Christ also loved the church and gave Himself for her, that He might sanctify and cleanse her with the washing of water by the word, that He might present her to Himself a glorious church, not having spot or wrinkle or any such thing, but that she should be holy and without blemish."

~ Ephesians 5:25-29

CHAPTER FOUR

The Motivation for Marriage

Marriage Is Too Sacred to Enter It for the Lust of the Eyes

And it came to pass, when men began to multiply on the face of the earth, and daughters were born unto them, that the sons of God saw the daughters of men that they were fair; and they took them wives of all which they chose. - Genesis 6:1

> *Moses does not deem it worthy of condemnation that regard was had to beauty, in the choice of wives; but that mere lust reigned. For marriage is a thing too sacred to allow that men should be induced to it by the lust of the eyes. For this union is inseparable comprising all the parts of life; as we have before seen, that the woman was created to be a helper of*

the man. Therefore our appetite becomes brutal, when we are so ravished with the charms of beauty, that those things which are chief are not taken into the account. Moses more clearly describes the violent impetuosity of their lust, when he says, that they took wives of all that they chose; by which he signifies, that the sons of God did not make their choice from those possessed of necessary endowments, but wandered without discrimination, rushing onward according to their lust. We are taught, however, in these words, that temperance is to be used in holy wedlock, and that its profanation is no light crime before God.[1]

Marrying for Beauty's Sake

And Jacob loved Rachel; and said, I will serve thee seven years for Rachel thy younger daughter. - Genesis 29:18

Further, it is not altogether to be deemed a fault that Jacob was rather inclined to love Rachel; whether it was that Leah, on account of her tender eyes, was less beautiful, or that she was pleasing only by the comeliness of her eyes, while Rachel excelled her altogether in elegance of form. For we see how naturally a secret kind of affection produces mutual love. Only excess is to be guarded against, and so much the more diligently, because it is difficult so to restrain affections of this kind, that they do not prevail to the stifling of reason. Therefore he who shall be induced to choose a wife, because of the elegance of her form, will not necessarily sin, provided reason always maintains the ascendancy, and holds the wantonness of passion in subjection.[2]

“Let thy fountain be blessed: and rejoice with the wife of thy youth.”

~ Proverbs 5:18

CHAPTER FIVE

Necessary Age for Marriage

Children Getting Married

It has always been judged and rightfully so, that marriage is not legitimate except between those who have reached puberty. When a boy marries a girl, this is a childish game, and the sort of levity that deserved punishment.

First of all, it must be stated that those who are under the authority of their parents or guardians are not free or independent, especially in this matter. Even if the parents or guardians consent, or even if they are the principal instigators of the marriage—nonetheless, the contracts made before the proper age do not bind the children unless, after they reach puberty, they feel the same way, and voluntarily acknowledge that they consider their premature marriage valid.

If any parents betroth their children before they reach puberty, and pledge themselves and their possessions, they nevertheless cannot bind the children who are not yet ready for marriage. A contract of this sort is a profaning of marriage... The terms of marriage cannot be carried out, since the children, when they reach puberty, are free to retract whatever their parents wrongfully contracted on their part.[1]

On Older Men Marrying Younger Women

If a decrepit old man falls in love with a young girl, it is because of his base and shameful lust. He will defraud her if he marries her.[2]

"So Abraham said to the oldest servant of his house, who ruled over all that he had, 'Please, put your hand under my thigh, and I will make you swear by the Lord, the God of heaven and the God of the earth, that you will not take a wife for my son from the daughters of the Canaanites, among whom I dwell; but you shall go to my country and to my family, and take a wife for my son Isaac.'"

~ Genesis 24:2-4

CHAPTER SIX

Parental Consent

Children Who Commit to Marriage without Parental Consent

And Abraham said unto his eldest servant of his house, that ruled over all that he had, Put, I pray thee, thy hand under my thigh: And I will make thee swear by the LORD, the God of heaven, and the God of the earth, that thou shalt not take a wife unto my son of the daughters of the Canaanites, among whom I dwell: But thou shalt go unto my country, and to my kindred, and take a wife unto my son Isaac. - Genesis 24:2-4

> *Now this example should be taken by us as a common rule, to show that it is not lawful for the children of a family to contract marriage, except with the consent of parents; and certainly natural equity dictates*

that, in a matter of such importance, children should depend upon the will of their parents. How detestable, therefore, is the barbarity of the Pope, who has dared to burst this sacred bond asunder! Wherefore the wantonness of youths is to be restrained, that they may not rashly contract nuptials without consulting their fathers.[1]

The Duty of Parents to Assist in Children's Marriages

And Abraham said unto his eldest servant of his house, that ruled over all that he had, Put, I pray thee, thy hand under my thigh. - Genesis 24:2

Abraham here fulfils the common duty of parents, in laboring for and being solicitous about the choice of a wife for his son: but he looks somewhat further; for since God had separated him from the Canaanites by a sacred covenant, he justly fears lest Isaac, by joining himself in affinity with them, should shake off the yoke of God.[2]

The Marriage of a Rebellious Child

Fathers or guardians shall not have marriages contracted for their children or wards until they have reached an age to confirm them. Nevertheless, if it happens that a child, having refused to marry according to the will of his father, thereafter chooses a marriage that is not so much to his profit and advantage, because of such rebellion or defiance the father shall not be required to give him anything during his [the father's] lifetime.[3]

On Excessively Strict Parents

Where children marry without their father's or mother's permission at the age permitted... and it is established by the court that they have done this lawfully because of the negligence or excessive strictness of their fathers, let the fathers be required to grant them a dowry or provide them such a share or position as [they would have given] if they had consented to it.[4]

"So they said, "We will call the young woman and ask her personally." Then they called Rebekah and said to her, "Will you go with this man?" And she said, "I will go."

~ Genesis 24:57-58

CHAPTER SEVEN

Necessity of Individual Consent

A Daughter's Willing Consent

And Caleb said, He that smiteth Kirjath-sepher, and taketh it, to him will I give Achsah my daughter to wife. And Othniel the son of Kenaz, the brother of Caleb, took it: and he gave him Achsah his daughter to wife. - Joshua 15:16-17

> *Although it is the office of parents to settle their daughters in life, they are not permitted to exercise tyrannical power and assign them to whatever husbands they think fit without consulting them. For while all contracts ought to be voluntary, freedom ought to prevail especially in marriage that no one may pledge his faith against his will... It seems to me, however, that according to common law, the*

agreement implied the daughter's consent, and was only to take effect if it was obtained. God certainly heard the prayer of Caleb, when he gave him a son-in-law exactly to his mind. For had the free choice been given him, there was none whom he would have preferred.[1]

On Forced Marriages

Let no father compel his children to such a marriage as seems good to him except with their goodwill and consent, but let him or her who does not want to accept the partner his father wants to give be excused, always preserving modesty and respect, without the father imposing any punishment for such a refusal. The same shall be observed for those under guardianship.[2]

Punishment for Deception

If it is found that there has been some deception or that anyone, man or woman, has induced them to do this, let the punishment be three days on bread and water and to beg mercy before the court of those who are affected.

Let the witnesses who were involved in making such a marriage also be punished with prison for one day on bread and water.[3]

"None of you shall approach anyone who is near of kin to him, to uncover his nakedness: I am the Lord."

~ Leviticus 18:6

CHAPTER EIGHT

Marriage within Families

Rules for Marriages within Families

In a direct line, that is of father with daughter or mother with son or all other descendents in order, no marriage may be contracted since this contravenes natural decency and is forbidden both by the law of God and by the civil law.

Likewise of uncle with [niece] or great-[niece], of aunt with nephew or great-nephew and so on, because the uncle represents the father and the aunt is in the place of the mother.

Also between brother and sister, whether of [the same] father and mother or of one of these.

In the other degrees, although marriage is not forbidden either by the law of God or the Roman civil law, nevertheless to avoid scandal, because for a long time this has not been the custom, and from fear that the Word of God may be blasphemed by the ignorant, a cousin-german [first cousin] may not contract marriage with his cousin-german until, with the passing of time, it is otherwise decided by us. To the other degrees let there be no impediment.[1]

On the Degrees of Affinity

Let no man take to wife the widow of his son, or of the son of his son, and let no woman take the husband of her daughter or of the daughter of her daughter, nor of those following traced down in a direct line.

Let no one take the daughter of his wife or the daughter descending from her, and so on.

A woman also may not take the son of her husband or the son of his son, and so on.

Likewise let no one take the widow of his nephew or of his great-nephew, and also let no woman take the husband of her niece or great-niece.

Let no one take the widow of his brother, and no woman may take the one who was her sister's husband.

The one who has committed adultery with the wife of another, when it has come to be known, may not take her in marriage because of the scandal and dangers this entails[2]

"Do not be unequally yoked together with unbelievers. For what fellowship has righteousness with lawlessness? And what communion has light with darkness?"

~ 2 Corinthians 6:14

CHAPTER NINE

Equal Yoking

Mixing with Idolaters in Marriage

As long as we live among unbelievers, we cannot escape those dealings with them which relate to the ordinary affairs of life; but if we approach nearer, so that a greater intimacy should arise, we open the door as it were to Satan... It is notorious that men are too apt to be led away by the blandishments of their wives; and also, that men in their power compel their wives to obedience. Those, therefore, who mix with idolaters, knowingly and willfully devote themselves to idols.[1]

What Does It Mean to Be Unequally Yoked

Be ye not unequally yoked together with unbelievers: for what fellowship hath righteousness with unrighteousness? And what communion hath light with darkness? - II Corinthians 6:14

> *Many are of opinion that he speaks of marriage, but the context clearly shows that they are mistaken. The word that Paul makes use of means — to be connected together in drawing the same yoke. It is a metaphor taken from oxen or horses, which require to walk at the same pace, and to act together in the same work, when fastened under one yoke. When, therefore, he prohibits us from having partnership with unbelievers in drawing the same yoke, he means simply this, that we should have no fellowship with them in their pollutions. For one sun shines upon us, we eat of the same bread, we breathe the same air, and we cannot altogether refrain from intercourse with them; but Paul speaks of the yoke of impiety,*

that is, of participation in works, in which Christians cannot lawfully have fellowship. On this principle marriage will also be prohibited, inasmuch as it is a snare, by which both men and women are entangled into an agreement with impiety; but what I mean is simply this, that Paul's doctrine is of too general a nature to be restricted to marriage exclusively, for he is discoursing here as to the shunning of idolatry, on which account, also, we are prohibited from contracting marriages with the wicked.[2]

"And what man is there who is betrothed to a woman and has not married her? Let him go and return to his house, lest he die in the battle and another man marry her.'"

~ Deuteronomy 20:7

CHAPTER TEN

Proposals of Marriage and Engagements

The Seriousness of the Marriage Proposal

Let all promises of marriage be made honorably and in the fear of God and not in dissoluteness or through reckless frivolity, as by merely offering a glass to drink together without previously having agreed in sober discussion, and let those who do otherwise be punished.[1]

Marriage Promises to Be Made Simply and Unconditionally

Although in discussing or arranging a marriage it is lawful to add conditions or reserve someone's consent, nevertheless when it comes to making the promise let it be pure and simple, and let a statement made conditionally not be regarded as a promise of marriage.[2]

Secret Promises of Marriage

Let no one make clandestine promises, conditionally or otherwise, between young people who have not yet been married, but let there be at least two witnesses; otherwise the whole [secret engagement] shall be void.[3]

Handling Disagreements over Promises of Marriage

If anyone takes another to court, alleging a promise of marriage, unless there are two respectable witnesses of good repute, let an oath be administered to the defendant, and on his denying the charge let him be absolved.[4]

The Length of Time Between the Promise of Marriage and the Wedding

After the promise is made, let the marriage not be delayed for more than six weeks; otherwise let the parties be called to the Consistory to be admonished. If they do not obey, let them be remanded before the Council to be compelled to celebrate it.[5]

Dealing with Outside Opposition to the Marriage

If there is any opposition [to the marriage], let the minister send the opponent before the Consistory on the earliest day and admonish him to have the accused party cited. However, let no one be received in opposition who is not of this city or otherwise known or accompanied by someone who knows him, to prevent others from causing blame or injury to some respectable girl, or the opposite.

If the opponent does not appear on the day he has been summoned, let the banns and the marriage proceed as if no impediment had arisen.[6]

Admitting Foreigners in Marriage

To avoid all the frauds that are committed in these matters, let no foreigner coming from a distant country be admitted to marriage unless he has good and certain testimony, either by letters or by respectable people, worthy of faith, that he has not been married elsewhere, and also of his good and respectable behavior; and let the same be observed with respect to girls and women.[7]

Wedding Announcements

Let the [summons] be published for three Sundays in the church before the wedding is held, the signature of the first syndic being obtained beforehand to attest that the parties are known; nevertheless the wedding may be held on the third publication. And if one of the parties is from another parish, let there also be an affidavit from that place.[8]

Cohabitation after Engagement

During the engagement the parties shall not live together as man and wife until the marriage has been blessed in the church after the custom of Christians. If any are found who have done the contrary, let them be punished by prison for three days on bread and water and be called to the Consistory to be admonished for their fault.[9]

"After His mother Mary was betrothed to Joseph, before they came together, she was found with child of the Holy Spirit. Then Joseph her husband, being a just man, and not wanting to make her a public example, was minded to put her away secretly."

~ Matthew 1:18

CHAPTER ELEVEN

The Permanence of Engagements

Reasons a Promise May Be Withdrawn

Once it is established that a promise has been made between capable persons, the marriage shall not be dissolved except in [two] cases, that is when it is found by sufficient proof that a girl who was taken for a virgin is not one, or if one of the parties has a contagious and incurable bodily disease.

Failure to pay a dowry or money or provide an outfit shall not prevent the marriage from coming into full effect, since these are only accessory.[1]

Desertion of Fiancés or Fiancées

If a man, after having sworn faith [that is, become engaged] to a girl or woman, goes to another country, and the girl or woman comes to make a complaint about this, asking to be delivered from her promise because of the other's disloyalty, let inquiry be made whether he did this for an honorable reason and with the knowledge of his fiancée, or instead through debauchery and because he does not wish to complete the marriage. If it is found that he has no apparent reason [for his departure] and that he has done it from bad motives, let one inquire where he has gone, and if possible let him be notified that he must return by a certain day to carry out the duty he has promised.

If he does not appear, having been warned, let it be proclaimed for three Sundays in the church that he must appear, such that there is a gap of [two weeks] between two proclamations and thus that the whole term is six weeks. If he does not appear within the term, let the girl or woman be declared free and the man banished for disloyalty. If he appears, let him be compelled to celebrate the marriage the first day it can be done. If it is not known where he has gone and the girl or woman, along with his closest friends, swear they do not know [his whereabouts], let the same proclamations be made as if he had been notified, with the object of freeing her [from the engagement].

If he had some good reason and also informed his fiancée, let the girl or woman wait for the space of a year before proceeding against him in his absence, and meanwhile let the girl herself and her friends make diligent efforts to induce him to return. If after a year has passed he does not return, then let the proclamations be made in the manner described above.

Let the same course be observed against a girl or woman, except that the [prospective] husband shall not be required to wait a year even if she departed with his knowledge and consent, unless he gave her permission to make a journey that requires such a long absence.

If a girl duly bound by a promise is fraudulently transported outside the territory [of Geneva] in order not to complete the marriage, let one inquire whether there is anyone in the city who has aided in this so he may be compelled to make her return, under whatever penalty may be decided: or if she has guardians or trustees, let them likewise be enjoined to make her come back if they can.[2]

Dissolving Marriage Engagements

True and valid engagements cannot be dissolved any more than consummated marriages, since God's commands also apply here: "What God has joined together, let not man put asunder." They cannot be broken by mutual consent of both parties, far less by the will of either party as once was tolerated by the Romans, and even by Moses because of the stubbornness of the Jews.[3]

"Blow the trumpet in Zion, sanctify a fast, call a solemn assembly: Gather the people, sanctify the congregation, assemble the elders, gather the children, and those that suck the breasts: let the bridegroom go forth of his chamber, and the bride out of her closet"

~ Joel 2:15-16

CHAPTER TWELVE

The Marriage Ceremony

The Marriage Celebration - Conduct on the Wedding Day

When it is time for the parties to be married, let them come modestly to the church without drummers or fiddlers, preserving the order and gravity proper to Christians, and do this before the end of the tolling of the bell, so that the blessing of the marriage may take place before the sermon. If they are negligent and come too late, let the marriage be postponed.[1]

On What Days Can Marriages Be Consummated

It is permissible to celebrate marriages every day, that is on working days at the sermon that seems best to the parties, on Sunday at the sermon at dawn or at three in the afternoon, except on the days when communion is celebrated, so that then there may be no distractions and everyone may be better disposed to receive the sacrament.[2]

"Husbands, likewise, dwell with them with understanding, giving honor to the wife, as to the weaker vessel, and as being heirs together of the grace of life, that your prayers may not be hindered."

~ 1 Peter 3:7

CHAPTER THRITEEN

Post-Marriage Concerns

Dealing with Quarrels After the Wedding

If a husband does not live in peace with his wife, but they have conflicts and quarrels with each other, let them be summoned to the Consistory to be admonished to live in good concord and unity and each be remonstrated with for his faults according to the needs of the case.

If it is known that a husband mistreats his wife, beating and tormenting her, or that he threatens to do her an injury and is known to be a man of uncontrolled anger, let him be sent before the Council to be expressly forbidden to beat her, under pain of certain punishment.[1]

Handling Discoveries After the Wedding Day

If it happens that a woman complains that the one who has taken her in marriage is physically maimed and not able to have the company of a woman, and this is found true by confession or examination, let the marriage be declared void, the woman be declared free, and the man be forbidden to defraud any woman again.

Likewise if the man complains of not being able to have the company of his wife because of some defect in her body and she does not want to allow it to be cured, after the truth of the fact is established let the marriage be declared void.[2]

On Living Arrangements After Marriage

Let the husband have his wife with him and let them live in one house, maintaining a common household. If it happens that one withdraws from the other to live apart, let them be summoned to be admonished and be compelled to return to each other.[3]

Dealing with a Disappearance of Unknown Cause

If a man goes on a journey to deal in merchandise or otherwise without fraud or alienation from his wife, and he does not return for a long time and it is not known what has happened to him, so that by reasonable conjecture he is presumed dead, nevertheless let his wife not be permitted to remarry until after a term of ten years has passed since the day of his departure unless there is certain testimony of his death: which being received, one may give her permission. This permission [to remarry] after ten years, however, extends only to the point that if one suspects either from reports or evidence that the man is held prisoner or is hindered by some other obstacle, then let the wife remain in widowhood.[4]

Procedure for Dealing with a Husband's Abandonment

If a man through debauchery or some evil feeling goes away and abandons his place of residence, let his wife make diligent inquiry to learn where he has gone. Having learned where he is, let her come ask for official letters so she can summon him or otherwise compel him to do his duty, or at least notify him that he must return to his household under penalty of being proceeded against in his absence. If this is done and there is no way of compelling him to return, let one not fail to proceed as he was warned, that is, to proclaim him [a deserter] in the church for three Sundays, two weeks apart, so that the term is six weeks. Let the same be done three times in the Lieutenant's court, and let two or three of his closest friends, or relatives if he has them, be notified of this. If he does not appear, let his wife come to the next Consistory [meeting] to ask for a separation, and let it be granted to her, sending her before the Council [for them] to make a judicial decision about it. And let the one who has been so rebellious be banished forever. If he appears, let them be reconciled in good accord and in the fear of God.[5]

Dealing with Repeated Abandonment

If any man makes a habit of thus abandoning his wife to wander about the country, the second time let him be punished by imprisonment [on] bread and water, and let him be commanded with strong threats not to do so any more. The third time let greater rigor be employed against him, and if there is no improvement, let one provide that the wife is no longer bound to such a man, who gives her neither faith nor companionship.[6]

Dealing with Abandonment from Debauchery of a Husband

If a man, being debauched as aforesaid, has abandoned his wife without his wife having given him occasion or having been to blame, and this is duly established by the testimony of the neighbors and friends, and the wife comes to complain, asking for a remedy, let her be admonished to make diligent inquiry to find out what has become of him, and let his closest relatives and friends, if he has any, be summoned to get news from them. However, let the wife wait till the end of a year to see whether she cannot learn where he is, commending herself to God. At the end of the year, she may come to the Consistory, and if it is known that she needs to marry, after exhorting her let her be remanded to the Council to be asked on oath whether she knows where he has gone, and let the same be done to his closest relatives and friends. After this, proceed to the aforementioned proclamations to give the woman liberty to remarry. If the absent [husband] returns afterwards, let him be punished as one thinks reasonable.[7]

Dealing with Wives Who Abandon Husbands

If a wife departs from her husband and goes to another place and the husband comes to ask to be separated from her and set at liberty to remarry, let it be determined whether she is in a place from which she can be summoned or where she can at least be notified that she must appear to respond to her husband's request, and let the husband be aided with letters and other means to do this. If this is done, let one make such proclamations as were described above, having first summoned her closest relatives or friends to admonish them to make her return if they can. If she appears within the term and her husband refuses [to take her] because of the suspicion he has that she has mismanaged her body and because it is too scandalous a thing for a wife thus to abandon her husband, let one try to reunite them, exhorting the husband to pardon her fault. Nevertheless, if he persists in making an issue of this, let inquiry be made in the place where she was as to what people she associated with and how she behaved. If no certain evidence or proof is found to convict her of having breached marital faith, let the husband be compelled to be reconciled with her. If she is charged with a very strong presumption of having fornicated, as by having associated with bad and suspect company and not having maintained the proper behavior of a respectable woman, let the husband's request be heard and he be granted what reason justifies. If she does not appear during the term, let the same procedure be followed against her as against the husband in a similar situation.[8]

END NOTES

Chapter 2

1. Calvin, John, Institutes of the Christian Religion, trans. Henry Beveridge (eBook, Ages Bible Software 1998), S. IV, xiii, 21.
2. Calvin, John, Commentary on Genesis, Vol. 1, trans. John King (Grand Rapids, MI: Baker Books, reprinted 2003), 128-129.
3. Calvin, John, Commentary on the Corinthians, Vol. 1, trans. William Pringle (Grand Rapids, MI: Baker Books, reprinted 2003), 223-224.
4. Calvin, John, Commentary on the Gospel of John, trans. John King (eBook, Ages Bible Software, 1998), 68, 73.
5. Calvin, John, Institutes of the Christian Religion, trans. Henry Beveridge (eBook, Ages Bible Software 1998), S. IV, ix, 14.

Chapter 3

1. Calvin, John, Institutes of the Christian Religion, trans. Henry Beveridge (eBook, Ages Bible Software 1998), S. II, viii, 41.
2. Calvin, John, Commentary on Genesis, edited by John King (eBook, Ages Bible Software, 1998), 582.

Chapter 4

1. Calvin, John, Commentary on Genesis, Vol.1, trans. John King (Grand Rapids, MI: Baker Books, reprinted 2003), 154-155.
2. Calvin, John, Commentary on Genesis, Vol. 2, trans. John King (Grand Rapids, MI: Baker Books, reprinted 2003), 130.

Chapter 5

1. Witte, John Jr., and Kingdon, Robert M. Sex, Marriage, and Family in John Calvin's Geneva: Courtship, Engagement, and Marriage. Edited by Browning, Don and Witte, John Jr. (Grand Rapids, MI: Eerdmans Publishing Company, 2005), 44. Original source, Calvin, John, Consilium, translated in Calvin's Ecclesiastical Advice, 122-123.
2. Calvin, John, Harmony of the Law, Vol. 4, trans. Charles Bingham (Grand Rapids, MI: Baker Books, reprinted 2003), 31.

Chapter 6

1. Calvin, John, Commentary on Genesis, trans. John King (eBook, Ages Bible Software, 1998), 429.
2. Ibid., 427.
3. Witte, John Jr., and Kingdon, Robert M. Sex, Marriage, and Family in John Calvin's Geneva: Courtship, Engagement, and Marriage. Edited by Browning, Don and Witte, John Jr (Grand

Rapids MI: Eerdmans Publishing Company, 2005), 53.

4. Ibid., 52.

Chapter 7

1. Calvin, John, Commentary on Joshua, trans. Henry Beveridge (Grand Rapids, MI: Baker Books, reprinted 2003), 93-94.
2. Witte, John Jr., and Kingdon, Robert M. Sex, Marriage, and Family in John Calvin's Geneva: Courtship, Engagement, and Marriage. Edited by Browning, Don and Witte, John Jr (Grand Rapids MI: Eerdmans Publishing Company, 2005), 53.
3. Ibid., 52.

Chapter 8

1. Witte, John Jr., and Kingdon, Robert M. Sex, Marriage, and Family in John Calvin's Geneva: Courtship, Engagement, and Marriage. Edited by Browning, Don and Witte, John Jr (Grand Rapids MI: Eerdmans Publishing Company, 2005), 55-56.
2. Ibid., 56.

Chapter 9

1. Calvin, John, Harmony of the Law, Vol. 2, edited by the Rev. Charles William Bingham (eBook, Ages Bible Software, 1998),

251-252.

2. Calvin, John, Commentary on the Corinthians, Vol. 2, trans. William Pringle (Grand Rapids, MI: Baker Books, reprinted 2003), 257-258.

Chapter 10

1. Witte, John Jr., and Kingdon, Robert M. Sex, Marriage, and Family in John Calvin's Geneva: Courtship, Engagement, and Marriage. Edited by Browning, Don and Witte, John Jr (Grand Rapids MI: Eerdmans Publishing Company, 2005), 53.
2. Ibid., 54.
3. Ibid., 52.
4. Ibid., 53.
5. Ibid., 54.
6. Ibid.
7. Ibid.
8. Ibid., 55.
9. Ibid.

Chapter 11

1. Witte, John Jr., and Kingdon, Robert M. Sex, Marriage, and Family in John Calvin's Geneva: Courtship, Engagement, and Marriage. Edited by Browning, Don and Witte, John Jr (Grand

Rapids MI: Eerdmans Publishing Company, 2005), 53-54.

2. Ibid., 59-60.
3. Witte, John Jr., and Kingdon, Robert M. Sex, Marriage, and Family in John Calvin's Geneva: Courtship, Engagement, and Marriage. Edited by Browning, Don and Witte, John Jr (Grand Rapids MI: Eerdmans Publishing Company, 2005), 44. Original source, Calvin, John, sermon on Deut 22:25-30.

CHAPTER 12

1. Witte, John Jr., and Kingdon, Robert M. Sex, Marriage, and Family in John Calvin's Geneva: Courtship, Engagement, and Marriage. Edited by Browning, Don and Witte, John Jr (Grand Rapids MI: Eerdmans Publishing Company, 2005), 55.
2. Ibid.

CHAPTER 13

1. Witte, John Jr., and Kingdon, Robert M. Sex, Marriage, and Family in John Calvin's Geneva: Courtship, Engagement, and Marriage. Edited by Browning, Don and Witte, John Jr (Grand Rapids MI: Eerdmans Publishing Company, 2005), 56.
2. Ibid., 57.
3. Ibid., 55.
4. Ibid., 57-58.

5. Ibid., 58.
6. Ibid.
7. Ibid.
8. Witte, John Jr., and Kingdon, Robert M. Sex, Marriage, and Family in John Calvin's Geneva: Courtship, Engagement, and Marriage. Edited by Browning, Don and Witte, John Jr (Grand Rapids MI: Eerdmans Publishing Company, 2005), 58-59.